Hood in the Woods

Vol I

By

Johnny Ashley

2020

ISBN

978-0-359-77073-1

Made in the USA
Charleston, SC
17 July 2013

FOSTER FALLS HOTEL, GIRLS INDUSTRIAL SCHOOL, AND ORPHANAGE

Many buildings have worn many hats; as times change so do needs and resources. A once thriving town can resort back to country, as is the case with Foster Falls. The company town that was once here is now cared for by the Virginia Park Services. The old Norfolk and Western (before they became Norfolk and Southern) railroad line is now a trail that runs through several counties.

An Iron furnace was constructed in Foster Falls (Wythe County, VA) in 1881, and by 1895 the population was 296 people. Besides the hotel, there was also a grist mill, sawmill, distillery, and nearly 100 houses. Foster Falls, located on the bank of the New River, a usually slow and lazy river. But it moves fast here, which makes the area prime for hydro powered mills.

The hotel, which opened in 1888, was built as soon as the railroad line reached Foster Falls. Both the town and hotel were built by the Foster Falls Mining and Manufacturing company. The Hotel was built as the centerpiece of the Foster Falls community. Not only as a hotel, it also served the community as the post office, saloon and company offices.

In 1916 the furnace's fires burned out, and the population declined. As people left and businesses closed, there was no need for the ornate Victorian hotel. In 1919 ownership of the hotel was transferred to the Abingdon Presbytery Church for only one dollar. The church used the hotel as an industrial school for girls, which hosted girls aged 14-20 studying a wide range of subjects, from accounting to geography.

    In 1938 the building changed purpose and name again. This time it became a co-ed orphanage. It's important to remember that this was during the great depression, when extreme poverty gripped the United States. It's sad but true; some families simply couldn't care for their children. The most they could do for them, was to leave their children at an orphanage or an asylum. Safety was never guarantied, but at least here they would know that their children had a meal to eat and a bed to sleep in.

In 1962 the hotel/school/orphanage was badly burned in a fire; the children were relocated, and the building was closed.

Along with the old railroad line, it was purchased by the state in 1986.

Although the state has been repairing and renovating since then, it is still a work in progress.

THE FOSTER FALLS IRON FURNACE

As previously mentioned, the furnace was built in 1881 by the Foster Falls Mining and Manufacturing Company. In 1887 a train bridge was built over the New River, connecting Foster Falls with nearby Hematite (iron ore) mines.

The furnace originally operated using water pressure from the New River to force air into the fire. In 1889 it was sold to the Virginia Coal and Coke Company. To improve production, they switched to a steam operated boiler in a process we today know as hot blasting. At its peak, the furnace produced 12 tons of steel a day. After a flood destroyed the bridge over the New River in 1916, the furnace was closed.

YELLOW SULFUR SPRINGS RESORT

Located down a forgotten dirt road in Montgomery County, Virginia, this healing springs resort was the spot where the who's who of yesteryear came to rub shoulders with each other and relax away from the public eye. Mineral rich water flows from rocks here, with a strong sulfur taste. Doctors would prescribe treatments which included drinking these waters rich in minerals, that freely flowed in southwest Virginia and southern West Virginia. Long before the arrival of the settlers, Native Americans came here for the same reason.

The earliest records show an Inn on this land in the 1700's. The main building was built by Charles Taylor in 1810 and expanded in 1840. Known as Taylor Springs, it was part of a mineral spring circuit in Virginia and West Virginia made by the wealthy.

The trend was started by Dr. William Burke who had visited nearby Red Sulfur Springs. Arriving weak and frail, he left fit and strong. He subsequently published multiple books on the healing powers of mineral springs in western Virginia. (The state of West Virginia did not exist at that time.) Dr. Burke eventually purchased Red Sulfur Springs, which is in Monroe County, West Virginia.

Gazebo built in 1870

Armistead Forrest purchased the springs in 1842 and added several free-standing cottages as well as additional cottage rows.

In 1853 he sold it to Foulks, Gardner and Edmundson, who changed the resort's name to Yellow Sulfur Springs. The resort closed during the Civil War; when it reopened in 1868, it became more popular than it was before.

Historian Charlene Lewis said that during the pre and post-civil war era "more southern elites congregated here than anywhere else in the south".

Southern Generals Judal Early and P.G.T Beauregard both had rooms reserved year-round for them.

In 1871 Yellow Sulfur was sold to James and John Wade, who built a second, larger hotel, which burned down two years later. In 1886 Ridgeway Holt bought the resort and rebuilt the second hotel in 1888. The new hotel had 60 guest rooms and a grand ballroom, as well as a 2-acre boating pond. The following year he built a bowling alley. At its peak, the resort could hold 400 people.

Partially due to advances in modern medicine, the mineral springs' fad began to fade. In addition, as automobiles became more common and rail traffic decreased, railroad destinations suffered. Yellow Sulfur was not spared the fate that befell the industry. It passed through multiple more hands.

The 1920's was a prosperous time for America's black citizens. The Harlem Renaissance was in full swing and throughout the country, many African Americans experienced increased prosperity. They began a new trend of visiting mineral spring resorts but were limited to only those that allowed black guests during the Jim Crow segregation era.

In 1926, a company founded by 10 African American businessmen from Roanoke purchased Yellow Sulfur Springs. Despite being well funded, the venture couldn't overcome the Great Depression, which took no prisoners.

It was sold at auction on the courthouse steps in 1929. During the Great Depression, the resort was leased by the Virginia Transit Bureau to retrain transients, and in the process restore the hotel. In the 1930's they installed the tin roof that is currently on the hotel. There are multiple unexplained foundations on the property that are believed to be a product of the retraining program.

When the depression ended, the resort was owned by Charles Crumpacker. After he died, his daughter Charlsie "Pistol Packing Mama" Crumpacker inherited the resort and lived there until her death. With Crumpacker's approval, the trainees were allowed to stay after the depression ended.

In 1960 the second hotel was torn down due to disrepair. In 1994 a tree fell on the bowling alley. In 1997 one of the cottage rows was torn down due to disrepair, and the carriage house burned down. In 1998 The owners replaced the hotel's foundation with cinder blocks.

The property is currently owned by Benard Ross and Victoria Taylor, who run a spa on the property. They have also renovated two of the cottage rows, totaling 12 rooms, which are currently rented out. They are very nice people.

COMPANY TOWN, UNIONS, AND THE COAL WARS

This is the Pocahontas Fuel Company Store in Boissevein, Virginia. In 1884, the first company store in southwestern Virginia and south West Virginia was opened by the Southwest Virginia Improvement Company in nearby Pocahontas, Virginia. In 1907 they joined with other mine owners to form the Pocahontas Fuel Company. Bituminous coal was mined here; it is some of the highest grade in the world.

Immigrants from all over the world, as well as African Americans from deeper in the south, came here to work in the booming coal economy. Initially, workers could deduct company store purchases from their paycheck. The system later changed to wage payment by company script, redeemable only when spent within the company. That included everything from paying your rent and bills, to buying food or going to the doctor. Outside of the company, the script had no monetary value.

The quality and price of the goods in the stores was very important. There was no free market in a company town, and some companies would overcharge for subpar goods. Some companies would often charge more for room and board than they paid the miners, which could easily force a miner into debt. Once in debt, a miner could be held in the coal camp until their debt was paid; this unfortunately resulted in miners incurring more debt for living expenses. Private detectives like the Baldwin-Felts of Roanoke, were hired to keep miners in debt from leaving the camp. Every miner lived in a home rented from the company. This lack of home ownership prevented generational wealth and kept miners and their families tied to the company.

Company towns operated with no elected local government, and often county and state officials cooperated fully with the mining companies.

Although mining safety has improved, even today mining is dangerous. Natural gasses can cause explosions or suffocation. But in a time before OSHA and labor laws, mining was a very dangerous industry. It was cheaper to hire a new worker than to improve safety conditions. Families were evicted from their homes when the miner of the household was killed in a mine accident.

Not all mine companies treated their employees the same. Some miners were very content in the way they were treated by their employer. That said, one practice applied to all company towns, eviction upon death. In 1920, 80% of miners in West Virginia lived in company towns.

Tensions simmered, strikes began and the United Mine Workers Union came to the coal fields. Mine companies fought tooth and nail against unionization. It was common for any miner who joined the union to be evicted from their home. Sometimes, mine companies would fire their entire staff and bring in a new group.

As the number of strikes increased, the Baldwin-Felts detectives began specializing in strike busting. In one case, the mine company gave in to the strikers' demands of more pay, but then doubled the cost of rent and products in its store.

During another strike, miners and their families were sleeping on the train track to prevent shipments of coal from leaving. The Baldwin-Felts detectives ran a train down the line killing and maiming those in its way.

This led to several armed confrontations. The notorious battle in this region occurred two counties away, in Matewan, West Virginia. It was a company town owned by the Stone Mountain Coal Corporation. In 1920, the police chief of Matewan was Sid Hatfield, appointed by Mayor Testerman. It was before his time, but he was a descendant of the Hatfield and McCoy Feud. Hatfield had previously been a coal miner, and he and Testerman were sympathetic to their cause. When the company wanted to put machine guns in the town, Hatfield told them no. The company was not used to being told no.

On May 21, 1920, 13 Baldwin-Felts detectives arrived on a train from Bluefield. Two of the Felts brother were among them. They were met at the station by Fred Burgraff, the Mingo county sheriff. They spent their day evicting several miner's families from their houses for joining the union.

There is no explanation as to why the Mingo county sheriff would be with the Felts brothers if the warrant was out his county. Sid Hatfield never was prosecuted for the warrant the Felt's brother produced for his arrest. If the detectives were only there to evict families from their homes, why did they carry machine guns in suitcases? Did they expect to be surrounded by armed miners? Were the miners instructed to arrive armed or were these evictions the tipping point? History's mysteries.

No one knows who fired the first shot. We do know that Testerman was the first one shot, followed by Hatfield shooting lead detective Albert Felts. The dusty street was filled with smoke as a running gun battle ensued. As the detectives ran back to the train station, they were ambushed on all sides by armed miners. Hatfield chased down Lee Felts, found him hiding in the post office, and killed him.

When the smoke cleared, seven detectives where dead, including both Felts brothers, and another one wounded. Testerman lay dying. Two miners were killed and other four wounded. One of the miners, Bob Mullins had been evicted from his house by the detectives earlier in the day. The other was Tot Tinsley, an unarmed bystander. The Governor ordered the state police to take control of Matewan. Sid Hatfield stacked the police department guns in the hardware store.

Sid Hatfield faced a slew of criminal charges stemming from the incident but was found not guilty by a Mingo county jury made up of his coal mining peers. This enraged the Baldwin-Felts detectives and made Hatfield a hero. The efforts to unionize increased.

The following year, Sid Hatfield was indicted in neighboring McDowell county for shooting up the tipple of a non-union mine. Sherriff Bill Hatfield guarantied the safety of Sid Hatfield and his deputy when they went to McDowell, but they were gunned down on the steps of the McDowell courthouse by Baldwin-Felts detectives.

ST. ALBANS SANATORIUM

Built on a bluff in Pulaski county, Virginia, across the New River from the City of Radford, stands this large empty building. Some say it's haunted because of its time as a mental hospital. Others say it's haunted by the ghost of boys who died there when it was a boarding school. Some say that it is built on haunted land.

The proximity to the river attracted both Native Americans and settlers. In July 1755, a group of Shawnee raiders attacked the settlement in Draper's Meadow in present day Radford. They killed at least five settlers and took the survivors as captives. The Shawnees and their captives regrouped and rested on the bluff where the empty building stands before making their way back to Ohio. Mary Draper Ingles was one of the prisoners. She was eight months pregnant, and earlier that day watched her family be killed or captured. She would later be sold into slavery, escape and follow the New River home.

During the Civil war, the union army used the bluffs above Radford to launch an artillery barrage on the town. The target was the depot of the Tennessee and Virginia Railroad. This line was vital to the south, running from Lynchburg, Virginia to Bristol, Tennessee.

Besides moving troops and supplies, the railroad also moved raw materials from the mineral rich mountains it traveled through. Like the five million tons of lead used to make bullets from nearby Ivanhoe, Virginia, and salt from Saltville, Virginia.

The bluff which St. Albans sits is treated to ghostly gunshots and smells of powder. Some people have even claimed to see ghostly figures running through the woods.

In 1892 George W. Miles Jr. was only 30 years old but had been a professor for ten years at Emory and Henry College. He saw how schools where run and wanted to try running his own. He founded a school which held fifty students and 4 teachers and named it the Lutheran's Boys School.

The teachers were the cream of the crop, and the stated goal of the school was to turn the boys into southern gentlemen and prepare them for the finest colleges. The school also encouraged competitive athletics. They played against nearby Virginia Tech in 1892 in Virginia Tech's first football game. Tech won 14-10.

The competitive atmosphere encouraged bullying. The strong making the weaker tough was encouraged. Things got out of hands a few times, leading to multiple homicides and suicides. One student died at his home during Christmas break from injuries he received here.

After George Miles died in 1903, without him leading the school, it closed eight years later in 1911. In 1915 the school and its 56 acres were bought by Dr. John King. He had used $500 of his own money and formed a corporation to borrow another $16,000. He renovated it and renamed it St. Albans.

He had previously been the superintendent at the Southwestern Lunatic Asylum and was appalled at the living conditions and treatment of patients. At St. Albans, patients were to be treated with dignity and respect. Not only would they eat fresh food, grown on the farm on the grounds but also work the farm as a chance exercise and socialize. When it first opened, it also served the community as a general hospital.

During the great depression, the patients where some of the best fed people around because of the farm. By 1945, 65,090 patients had come through St. Albans' doors, which was operated by only 48 staff members. Although Dr. King had his patients' best interest in mind, early treatments for the mentally ill were like medieval tortures.

Things like hydrotherapy, where patients would be submerged in ice water for days. Or wrapped up in towels dripping wet with ice cold water. Or even sprayed with a fire hose. The idea was that the cold water slowed the blood flow to the brain.

Another treatment of the era was insulin therapy, used on patients with schizophrenia. Small doses of insulin would be administered and gradually increased until comas where induced. The comas would last an hour or so, but the treatments could continue for years, with hundreds of comas. The idea was that the insulin induced coma would reset the patient's brain.

Another common treatment was electroshock therapy. The technic was first used in 1938. An electric current was run through the patient's body, causing seizures. Electroshock theory is still used today but has been renamed Electroconvulsive therapy. It is still used because it is effective tool to treat mental illness after other methods have failed.

Unfortunately for the patients of St. Albans electroshock therapy was in its infancy and they were the guinea pigs who it was tested on. This is the room it was done in. Treatments where administered with no anesthesia. Too much electric current could cause the patient's body to contort violently, broken bones weren't unheard of.

The aftereffects weren't much better, after multiple treatments patients would have prolonged head aches and sever memory loss. The patients dreaded coming to this room.

If they brought you down here, would you cry, struggle? How many times have they done it? How many more times will they? They are holding you down, one on each arm. Are you lying on your back with a tear running sideway out of your eye? You're asking and begging them to stop, why won't they? They can see how it hurts you. They tell you to shut up, they are helping you. This is your fault, you're the one who's sick. You struggle and squirm, they place the electrodes on your head. You see the dial turn……

Experiences like this has led to this room being popular with ghost hunters. It is also very easy to find. Just go into the deeper darkest depts of the basement, and there it is.

The severely mentally ill were not the only residents at St. Albans as in modern mental health facilities. Orphans and unwed mothers could also be found here. St. Albans also acted as a poor house or a county home. That accompanied by the wide variety of reasons (and often ridiculous by today's standards) that people were declared mental ill led to a wide variety of people being housed together. The mothers and orphans mentioned above could be living right next to a severely mentally ill person who could be unstable or violent.

The top floor on the western side of the building was reserved for older woman after their husbands had died. To them St. Albans was a retirement home. They shared bathrooms like the one pictured to the left.

The bathroom the right is called the suicide bathroom, it's just down the hall from the bathroom above. There have been multiple suicides in here. This is also another favorite with ghost hunters.

One of the suicided was lady who was pregnant and had a miscarriage. Heartbroken she stashed her baby away in a jar. When the nurses found it, they took it way and she was even more heart broken. She ran into this bathroom and slashed her wrists with a piece of broken glass. She died in this bathroom.

There's also a bowling alley in the basement. It was for the doctors to socialize after work or a reward for a patient. While it was abandoned, local kids coming down here and spray painting their name on the wall was how you earned your stripes in high school.

There's another ghost that haunts the boiler room next to the boiling ally. He's called Smoky and people pay tribute to him by leaving him cigarettes. He's known for being a little handsy with the ladies.

St. Albans also ran a rehab for alcoholics, it was both in and outpatient. The outpatient was run like a methadone clinic. Every day people would come and get their doctor prescribed shots of whisky to keep the shakes away. During prohibition people came here to legally get alcohol.

There is no paperwork to prove it, but local legend is that Johnny Cash came here to dry out once. I'm not saying he did sit in those chairs in the picture to the righ. I'm not saying he didn't either.

St. Alban continued to grow. In 1960 it was officially recognized as a hospital. They expanded to other communities is Virginia and West Virginia. In the 1980 there was a large renovation to keep the building updated. By the late 1980's it was Virginias only non-profit full-service psychiatric hospital. Eventually St. Albans merged with Carilion Heath System and was relocated to a wing in a new hospital. The land was gifted to Radford University in 2004, who planned to tear it down. In 2007 demolition was stopped as the process of adding St. Albans to the historic registry began.

Today St. Albans is privately owned. It is open for history tours, ghost tours, and a haunted house in the fall. Lots of volunteers give their time to make the tours and haunted house possible. All the proceeds from the tours and haunted houses go to paying taxes and maintaining the building.

MIDDLE RUN SCHOOL
LEWIS COUNTY, WV
1983–1943

THE BAPTIST COLLEGE

Opened in 1901, it began as a private coed secondary (high) school. As public high schools became more common enrollment dropped. Until public schools became common, high schools where mostly private and students had to pay tuition.

In 1911 the Baptist Association took over the school in 1918 and they added college classes.

In 1924 this U-shaped building was built.

This is the theater. It was the crown jewel of the school. At one point a third of the students where voice talented and that allowed the school to perform operas

The people from the town would go up the hill to the school to watch the show. The annual shows for the public would draw a large crowd and pack the room. Now the seats are falling into the floor.

In the picture on the left you can see the projector hole in the back of the room. The theater was also a movie theater.

There were only 18 faculty members. 6 taught academics, 6 taught arts and music, and 3 taught manual/domestic skills, and of course bible classes.

The Great Depression hurt the school which was forced to merge with another nearby college in 1931, and the campus closed.

To the left is the grand staircase at the entrance. The large windows you see had 2 story stained glass windows. They were moved to the new college and are still in the library.

Another college operated here from 1932 to 1935. After that it sat empty.

From 1953 to 1980's it was a private Christian high school. The strict rules for the students made the school unpopular forcing its close.

In the 90's it was briefly used as apartments. It has sat empty since. This building was never out of debt.

The top two floors where rooms for the students to stay in. Water leaking from the ceiling drips through four floors until it reaches the basement. The piles of debris on the floor show where the ceiling is caving in.

The basement has a basketball court and more classrooms. I've been here a few times. Last time I was here half of the basement was inaccessible because the floor above the hallway was caved in. There's a chance no one will ever go into this room again.

I've watched this building crumble. Staircases are falling apart. Making parts of the building inaccessible.

To the right is a student's dorm room on the second floor. That's the 3rd floor falling in on top. The wooden trusses and slats have been left to the elements too long. Its best to only walk in the hallways.

The brick exterior was built to last and will outlive the inside of the building, give the false impression of grandeur when it's only a shell.

To the left is another stage. How many children stood up there with their whole life in front of them and just sang their hearts out?

This is a nurse's station from the school. It's sad to see a place that was once happy and full of life sit this way. How many conversations with the nurse?

My boots echo through the silence as I wander the hallways.

Watching the slow decay increase with time. I feel like I'm forced to watch a friend die, unable to help them. This building had cancer, but now its terminal.

To the right are testing stations with dividers, like at the DMV.

To the left are seats that will never be sat in again. They are down the hallway in the basketball court, past the cave. I might have been the last person to walk into that room.

Just because I never went to school here doesn't mean I can't learn here. What do I hear in the silence?

I've known many men who have had a rock-solid appearance. Solid on the outside, like the brick on the building.

Sometimes when you peak inside them, all you see is yesteryears grandeur. After the life that fills them leaves, like this building, inside they fall apart.

I had to jump over a hole in the floor with all my equipment to get this picture. I don't foresee myself coming back.

Maybe if I'm in the neighborhood I might stop in unannounced to check in on my old friend.

I think that might put me to ease, but not by seeing this glorious school again. It'll keeping me from losing the life inside of me. Make my heart race again while I listen to my boots echo in the empty halls.

DOLLY PARTON
QUEEN OF GETTING AND GIVING

Dolly was born January 19, 1946 in Sevier County TN. She was born in a one room cabin on the banks of the Little Pigeon River. Dolly was the 4th of 12 children. None of these houses have anything to do with her, nor are they in Sevier County.

Her father (Lee) was a sharecropper with no formal education and could neither read nor write but was no dummy and was known for being a shrewd businessman.

Her mother (Avie) was sickly due to multiple complications during multiple births. Nothing wrong with her mouth though, and she would entertain her children from her bed, singing them songs and passing down mountain lore. Dolly (yes, her birth name) credits her father's business savvy and her mother's entertainment skills on her success.

In the 50's her family bought a nearby farm on Locust Ridge, where she would spend most of her childhood. In the 70's she put out a song about growing up there called "My Tennessee Mountain Home". In the 1980's she bought back the property (it had been sold long ago).

Dolly began singing on radio stations at 10. At 13 she recorded her first album, played at the "Grand 'Ole Opry" where she met Johnny Cash. He had just put out his "Live from San Quinton" album and encouraged her to continue performing. She graduated high school in 1964 and moved to Nashville.

Now we all know about the music and movies, so let's just skip over to what she did with the money.

Sometimes people go Hollywood and they don't come back. Not this Hillbilly, she went Dollywood. The original amusement park was called the "Rebel Railroad", opened in 1961, and is in Sevier county. By the time Dolly bought it in 1986, the park had been passed thru several owners. Dolly expanded the land of the park and added more attractions. No one knew more than Dolly the economic hardships of east TN and she vowed to help her people.

Dollywood now has over 3,000 staff members and is the largest employer in the county. Dolly put Pidgeon Forge on the map and now Dollywood is the largest tourist destination in TN with 3 million visitors annually.

In 2016 wildfires did a number on East TN and Sevier County wasn't spared. Dolly Parton began the "My people fund", and over 9 million dollars where donated during a telethon she hosted. 875 residence of Sevier County and surrounding areas who had lost their homes in the fire where given $1,000 a month for 6 months.

The last months check was supposed to be doubled ($2,000), but because of the excess of funds, the checks where increased to $5,000 and then doubled to $10,000. 3 million dollars where still left in the fund, and Dolly donated that to the "Mountain tough" program to further help with recovery effort.

Besides that, she has multiple other charities and programs to help the people of the region. She has poured millions of dollars into eastern Tennessee and affected countless lives in a region that has traditionally been neglected.

THE NEW RIVER GORGE BRIDGE, WV

Built in 1977, the bridge turned a 44-minute drive up and down the mountain to less than a minute.

More importantly than shortening the drive, the straight shot replaced a road that wasn't accessible to semi-trucks. The road was far too curvy for the trucks to drive up and down.

For years it was the world's longest single arch bridge, 3030 feet. It was also the tallest bridge at 847 feet.

It's now the fourth longest in the world but the longest in the Western Hemisphere and 25th highest.

"GHOST TOWN" OF PAMPLIN CITY, VA

      First of all, Pamplin City isn't a real ghost town. It still has a post office and zip code. Over 200 people call Pamplin City home. But it's industry left, and a once bustling town is left with a boarded up downtown and multiple other signs on population decline.

      The land has been settled since the late 1700's. Thomas Merriman bought the land in the early 1800's. He built a home and owned a shoe shop. The first written record of a town being on the land was in the early 1820's. The town was called Merriman Shop.

In 1833 Nicolas Pamplin bought 29 acres of this land. In 1854 a representative from the Norfolk and Western railroad came looking for land for a rail project. Nicholas Pamplin donated a large tract of land for the project.

Norfolk and Western built a junction connecting two major lines. The boom town that quickly grew was named Pamplin City to honor Nicholas Pamplin for his donation.

Soon hotels, banks and stores lined the newly made downtown streets. Glorious new homes popped up and Pamplin City was a town.

49

The Pamplin Pipe Factory was built in 1880. It was once the world's largest producer of fire blasted clay smoking pipes. At peak production they produced over a million pipes a month. In the picture to the left, you can see the factory and the kiln used to cure the pipes. The company dissolved in 1952.

To the right are some pipes I saw in a window of a building downtown. Pipes like these have been found in archaeological sites around the country. The style of the pipes also helps date the archaeological site.

Pamplin City became a staging area for the coal pulled from the Appalachians before it was shipped to the coast. Likewise, all the people flooding in to work in the coal fields passed through Pamplin City.

The transcontinental railroad linking the east and west coast wasn't completed until 1869. Before 1869 everything that was shipped to California had to be loaded onto a boat and ship around South America. This is still almost 50 years before the Panama Canal was built.

The rails roads that connected to the coast would see massive amounts of products that were meant to be sent to the west coast. Lots of milled timber was shipped from the Appalachians as well as coal. Pamplin city was also connected to the southern agriculture areas and lots of textiles where shipped through Pamplin City.

Pamplin City declined with the railroad. Using federal historical grants, the depot was renovated. It's now the city offices and the library.

The old school wasn't as lucky and sits board up, sad and lonely. The population peaked in 1970 with 394 residents. In the 2010 census the population was 219. But... it still has a post office and a zip code, 23958. I can't call it a ghost town. It's a faded glory town, and hopefully like the depot, the glory is restored.

POCAHONTAS, VIRGINIA

In 1860 Andrew Stower oppearted a mill and a blacksmith shop. He used coal from an exposed coal vein as fuel for his blacksmith shop. A few years afer the civil war Jordan Nelson traded his farm in Boone county West Virginia, for Mr. Stowers 1,000 acres in Virginia.

Burning logs in fireplaces could be dangerous in those day, one stray spark could cause a house to burn down. Mr. Nelson developed a stove that could burn coal. He began selling his stoves and soon expanded his buisness to delivering coal to his customer's homes.

One day a man came from Bluefield and bought a wagon load of coal. Mr. Nelson's Aunt Bessie saw what was going on and she ran outside. She scolded him, fearing he was selling the coal too fast and that soon his supply would run dry.

In the late 1870's the Southwest Virginia Improvement Company bought 400 acres of Mr. Nelson's land for $1,932. Soon they bought the mineral rights to another 400 acres. This left Mr. Nelson with only 100 acres.

The town of Pocahontas began as a coal camp and was incorporated in 1881. In 1881 the closest road or rail was 50 miles away. Norfolk and Western completed the New River line in 1883, with Pocahontas being its most western stop.

Commercial shipping on the New River line began in 1883. The line was completed in May and by the end of the year 82,000 tons of coal had been shipped on it.

That same year the first coke ovens where built. There ended up being 200 of the beehive shaped ovens. Coke ovens are used to cook out the impurities in the coal to make it more suitable for use in foundries.

The next year in 1884 the Southwest Virginia Improvement Company opened the "Old Company Store". It was the first company store in the region and was the beginning of what would turn into common practice. The Old Company Store remained being the largest company store in the region. The store also accepted cash.

The Southwest Virginia Improvement Company also put individual lots of land up for sale. Entrepreneurs poured into this unsettled land. A large building boom began. They built large buildings with ornate details and opened general stores, drug stores and of course saloons. Residential lots were also sold. Compared to these other stores, the Old Company store carried superior quality goods, although it was more expensive.

The picture to the right was the Opera house. It was the first Opera house in the region. It was such a big deal that special trains would come from Bluefield West Virginia to bring spectators.

Also, in 1884, the first school was built. It was in a log cabin. Four churches sprang up, but they had stiff competition from the 20 saloons. Pocahontas earned a reputation as a rough place.

In 1907 the Southwest Virginia Improvement company merged with other local mine owners to form the Pocahontas Fuel Company. It is still in operation and is called The Consolidated Fuel Company. The picture to the left is the old Pocahontas Fuel company offices.

Mr. Nelson died in 1922 in Bluefield, West Virginia. He was penniless and had nothing to show for owning one of the world's richest coal fields.

The coal from the Pocahontas coal fields is some of the highest quality in the world. It was used to dig the Panama Canal, fire the furnaces during the industrial revolution and win two world wars. It was preferred by the US Navy for its ships. In 1949 the diesel engine began to gain popularity, beginning the phasing out of coal.

In 1938 the Pocahontas number 1 mine closed. It was turned into a museum to educate the public on coal mining. In 1954 the last coal mine in Pocahontas closed. It is pictured to the right.

The Old Company Store was in operation until 1980. It was kept open because there were other Consolidated Fuel Company mining operations in the area and the store never stopped receiving business until the other mines closed and the script system ceased.

In 2007 nature reclaimed the building and it collapsed. It was listed on the top ten endangered historical sites in Virginia. The only landmark that could be salvaged was the elevator, as seen in the picture to the left.

In 1920 the population of Pocahontas peaked at 3,775 and in 2010 the population was 389 people. 45.6% of them are over the age of 44. As the population ages, population decline will only increase. To be clear this is not a ghost town, the post office is still open, and the zip code is 24635.

THE POCAHONTAS CEMETERY

This Cemetery begin its life as a park. In March 1884 there was a large mine blast in the Pocahontas east mine. 114 men and boys were killed.

Of those killed, 65 were white with 26 of them being recent European immigrants. The remaining 49 men where African Americans who had moved from the deep south for a better life in the coal fields.

It was 23 years after the civil war and in what turned out to be a historic event the men were buried side by side regardless of race. This had never happened in Virginian history before.

There was no noble reason for this. The coal camps where segregated. Miners are going to need houses, segregating the town didn't mean building any less houses. They were not about to waste land for two separate cemeteries.

During the civil war West Virginia seceded from Virginia. The location of Pocahontas is surrounded on three sides by equally coal rich West Virginia. Coal miners from Mercer county and McDowell county West Virginia are also buried here.

During this time there was a mass influx of Elis Island immigrants. Many people came from different cultures to live the American dream of prosperity, working in the coal fields. Death doesn't care where you are from or how far you came to get here. They died like their American brothers in mine explosions, of black lung and the countless other ways death greets you.

Tombstones in this cemetery are written in Polish, Russian, Italian and Hebrew. Today it is the most diverse cemetery in Virginia. Most of the people in this cemetery died young and died traumatic deaths. Most likely this has led to the tales of spirts and the supernatural that guests to this cemetery claim to experience. Please remember that its illegal in Virginia to be in a cemetery after sunset.

JENKINJONES, WEST VIRGINIA

On the other side of the mountian from Pocahontas, sits JenkinJones, in McDowell county West Virginia. Its named after its founder and owner, Jenkin Jones. He was a true American success story.

The houses in the top picture where the mine's management's houses. They are on the road to the coal mine. They have also seen better days

Jenkin Jones was born in Glen Neath, Wales in 1839. He grew up poor. His father died when Mr. Jones was 8 and he was forced to work in coal mines. In 1863 at the age of 24 he immigrated to America and found work in the coal fields of Pennsylvania.

Jenkin Jones teamed up with John Freeman and opened several mines in Pennsylvania. In 1884 he leased 14,000 acres in McDowell county West Virginia and continued opening mines.

In 1912 the town of JenkinJones was founded and in 1917 the first mine opened. He merged with the Pocahontas Fuel company, and Norfolk and Western hauled his coal out. Jenkinjones doesn't have an ornate downtown like Pocahontas, it has a coal camp feel.

Jenkinjones ran on the company script system, but the town was known for having a high quality of life. Cinderblock and wood framed houses lined the streets. The picture to the right is the company store. It was built in 1917.

Unfortunately, Mr. Jones never saw one truck of coal leave the mine in the town named after him. He died of tuberculosis in 1916, a year before the first mine opened. The last mine closed in 1989.

The picture to the left is a view of the company offices from the company store. In 1992, 3 years after the mines closed, they were placed on the historical registry.

When the mines closed, the company worked with the residents of town, often selling or gifting people the homes that they lived in. In 1989 all the homes in Jenkinjones where still owned by the company.

Poverty, and population decline hit Jenkinjones hard after the mine closed. Since 2010 the population has dropped more than 50%. The current population is 122 people. The medium income is less than $10,000 and the medium home price is $22,000. Although other mines still operate in the area, no other form of employment has come here and even a trip to a store can be difficult. The closest Walmart is an hour away.

Don't feel bad for the residents of Jenkinjones, if they wanted to leave like all the others did, they would have. They are here because they want to be here. This is their home and they are proud of where they live. Most of the current population worked at the mine when it was still open, and it's their children and grandchildren who have left.

Some of those kids and grandkids only moved a county or two away. Many now live in my county, in Virginia. Ultimately the kids and grandkids have spread out as far and wide as the coal their grandparents pulled out of the ground here.

The picture to the right is where a mighty house once stood. Many old homes have been consumed by fire or reclaimed by nature. Once densely populated streets are now only chimneys sticking out of the grass. Ghostly reminders of the past.

Please, do not think Jenkinjones is a ghost town though. There is still an operating post office and the zip code is 24848.

THE FREE STATE OF MCDOWELL

    Welcome to McDowell county. This mural greets you upon entering McDowell county from Wyoming county West Virginia. There was no better way for me to show the glory of McDowell county in one picture. To the left stands a true McDowell resident, a coal miner covered in coal dust. Ethnically, is he white or is he black? It doesn't matter, everyone came out of the mines looking the same. Men of different races, ethnicities and backgrounds worked together underground, risking life and limb to provide for their families. The house next to the miner and the one across the street are both company houses, duplexes were common.

    To the far right is a ship. The US Navy was a large consumer of McDowell county coal. The soldiers under it honor all the men who lay down their shovels and picked up guns when their country asked them to. The Yellow building next to them is the Kimball War Memorial. It was built in the heart of the black community and honors the 1,500 African Americans from McDowell county who volunteered for world war one.

The county formed in 1858 as part of Virginia and became the most southern county in West Virginia when the state split in 1863. The county seat was moved multiple times before settling in Welch in 1892. Welch was named after a civil war captain who surveyed the county and discovered coal. The empty downtown of Welch is pictured to the left.

During the coal boom of the industrial revolution, immigrants flocked here. This earned Welch the nickname Little New York. To this day many first-generation immigrants still live in McDowell county.

During that same boom, many African Americans flocked to the coal fields seeking a better life than they would have in the deep south. McDowell county still has the highest percentage of African American residents in West Virginia. Most notably, the "King of Comedy" Steve Harvey was born in Welch.

The Picture to the left shows a street that was once full of company homes, only two remain. Company towns operated in McDowell county for 100 years, ending in the 1980's.

Coal companies controlled all the local politics and often company towns would have no publicly elected officials. Although many people remember the glory of the mining days, everything was controlled by the mine companies. It doesn't matter how ethical they tried to be, they were businesses operating to turn a profit, and profits come before people.

There was little local government elected by the people for the people. Even standard utilities like water and power were provided by coal companies and not the county or state.

The Picture to the right is the Powerhouse. The first power plant was built by the Pocahontas Fuel company. Its located in Switchback. Its main goal was to provide power to the mines. It has been sold to the Appalachian Electric Power and now sits empty.

All the electricity used to mine in McDowell now comes from the Claytor Lake hydroelectric Dam, located in Pulaski county Virginia. The dam is also owned by Appalachian Electric Power.

Pictured to the left, the first water treatment plant in McDowell county was built in 1960 by the US Steel Company in Wilcoe. That's the same year that JFK came to tour poverty in the region.

When JFK toured McDowell, there was no hiding the poverty and desperation that effected the community. His expensive shoes were covered in mud as he walked the dirt streets of the coal camps. Many families lived as they did in the 1800's without power and clean water.

Coming from a well to do family this shocked him to his core. He came here to see it, but was he ready to see it and what would he do now that he had seen it?

To the right is five houses, one of them is occupied.

After you see parents not eating so their kids can, or starving children wearing rags playing in a mud street, you can't unsee that. He saw a standard of poverty that should have been unheard of during the postwar economic boom of the 1950's.

These people had been vital to the growth of the country and now that same country had turned its back on them. What JFK did would change American society forever and introduced a new term that is now very common. When elected he created food stamps.

The first recipients of modern-day food stamps were Chloe and Alderson Muncy of McDowell county. They received $95 for their 15 person house hold.

If you give a man a fish he'll eat for a day, if you teach him to fish, he'll eat every day. Many McDowell residents decided they would rather fish than be given fish and the mass exodus began.

In 1950 the population of McDowell county was 100,000 people. Currently it is less than 20,000. Only 1/5 of the former population remains there.

This exodus caused unexpected issues. School districts and towns reconsolidated. To the left is Switchback Elementary, it was a high school before that. It was built in 1924 and closed in 2004. Only memories wander the halls now. It doesn't have any windows because when it closed the school district took them out to use on another school.

In 1950 the coal industry employed 18,000 people in McDowell. That was 65% of the working age population. They didn't all work as miners, some worked for the rail roads, some maintained the trucks used to pull coal out of the mines. Even working in a company store was working in the coal industry.

To the right, while the house burned down the stone steps leading to it still stand, almost like a memorial. Nature is reclaiming the memorial, as nature reclaims all.

Free trade is good for the American consumer but not good for the American producer. As time passed and more steel mills closed so did coal mines. One steel mill in Gary Indiana closed in the 1980's and trickledown effect cost McDowell 1,200 jobs.

Business like the one to the left, sit empty. They left like everyone else.

Even during the best of times, life was always hard in McDowell county. Due to its remote location, technology and innovation passed over McDowell county. This has led to negative stereotypes and distain. In turn the residents of McDowell have had to rely on each other. The atmosphere has earned it the nickname The Free State of McDowell.

Today McDowell county, and coal country as a whole, have been reduced to nothing more than a political talking point. It's not a good talking point either. Politicians and talking heads on tv never say what can we do to help these people. No, they are singled out, pointed at and ridiculed.

Gary Indiana and Gary West Virginian were both company towns owned by US Steel. The West Virginia town mined the coal that was used in the Indiana's town's furnaces. The rust belt of the Midwest were the manufacturing centers fueled by Appalachian coal. They walked to their fates hand in hand. Their fates were no different but the response to their fates is very different from politicians and news casters.

The question must be asked. What will we as country do with places like McDowell county? Most of the population are people have lived there for their whole lives, worked the mines and now are retired or close to it. Most of the younger generation has left. There is little opportunity for them. When the aging current population that doesn't want to leave starts to die out, what will be left of McDowell? The pensions they receive are vital tax revenue for the county.

To the right is Big Creek Elementary school. Will McDowell continue to turn into burnt out ruins? Homer Hickam went to school here. He was America's first rocket scientist. He has been an outspoken critic of the treatment of McDowell but his story represents part of the problem in McDowell. He was the best and brightest and he left to chase his dreams, but no one replaced him, they followed him.

In 20 years will McDowell be an uninhabited wilderness again?

BRAMWELL, WEST VIRGINIA

A stone's throw outside of McDowell in Mercer county West Virginia sits the town of Bramwell. Bramwell is called the home of the millionaires. It was the choice town for coal barons to live in. Close enough they could easily make personal appearances at the mines but far enough away that they could be isolated from their employees' hardships.

Founded in 1889, more millionaires lived here per capita than anywhere else in the United States. During that time 17 millionaires called Bramwell home. In the early 1900's 13 called it home. The Bramwell bank was the wealthiest per capita in America.

Built on a horseshoe bend on the Bluestone river, the town is named after J.H. Bramwell. He was from Staunton Virginia and educated in civil engineering in NYC. In 1873 he accompanied captain Welch on his survey of the coal fields. Mr. Bramwell became a superintendent at the Flat Top Coal company and later the general manager of the Crozier coal and coke company. There were 38 coal mines in the Flat Top fields.

Mr. Bramwell was the town's first postmaster starting in 1883. He got rich selling lots of land in the town. The Pocahontas coal company, which employed 100,000 workers locally, had its main offices in Bramwell. At one-point Bramwell had 3 post offices within its limits.

In 1910 a fire started in a pool hall that burned down 21 buildings. The town was rebuilt, with lots of buildings being rebuilt with brick.

The fortunes of the town rose and fell with the coal industry. In 1984 the entire town was placed on the historic registry.

The central location of Bramwell has breathed new life into the town. It is now a popular tourist destination. Coal Barons mansions have been converted into B and B's. There are lots of ATV trails in the area and people flock to ride the dirt tracks.

The population of the town peaked at over 4,000 but in the 2010 census the population was 364 residents. Bramwell is not a ghost town and still has a functioning post office, its zip code is 24715.

THE TRANS-ALLEGHANY LUNATIC ASYLUM, WESTON, WEST VIRGINIA

This large asylum is listed on the Historical Registry but the treatment (or mistreatment) of the mentally ill was going on here before it was built. The previous buildings did not fit the needs of the community and a larger building was needed.

This is the world's second largest stone cut building in the world, behind the Kremlin in Russia. Skilled stone masons where imported from Ireland and Germany to help construct it.

The section in the picture above was for administration. It divided the hospital in half, with wings coming off in either direction. This style of asylum is called the Kirkbride design and can be found throughout the US.

It follows in the footsteps of the tuberculosis hospitals. The idea is that sunlight and fresh air can cure what ails you. I'm sure sunlight doesn't work as well as modern medicine, but I don't think they were wrong either. The asylum isn't very wide, only a hallway with rooms on either side. This ensured that every room would get a healthy dose of sunlight. Separate wings came of the back of the building to form court yards, like the picture to the left.

It was built between 1858 and 1881, with construction stopping during the civil war. The north set up an army base here, called Camp Tyler. They used the finished hospital ward as barracks. It was raided by the south twice during the civil war.

The first time (1862) the soldiers stole all the patient's blankets. The town got together and donated blankets to the hospital. The second time the south came (1863), they destroyed a ward of the hospital.

They began admitting patients in 1864, before it was completed. It was officially called the West Virginia Hospital for the Insane. The year before West Virginia had become its own state.

There were other buildings on the campus, all providing medical care if not working directly with mental health. A building is a building and as times changed so did needs. The building above was a tuberculosis hospital. It was built in 1935. After a cure was discovered it was converted into a hospital for the criminally insane.

The hospital was built to house 250 patients. Each was to have a room of their own and receive plenty of staff attention. A farm was also put on the over 600-acre campus so that the hospital could be self-sustaining.

Within 4 years they reached capacity, but the flow of people didn't stop. Modern mental health issues were not a requirement for commitment. Any flaw a man found in his wife could be a committable offense, and same goes parents bringing their children here. Lots of people with learning disabilities people were dropped off here. Orphans and unwed mothers would also be sent here. The same applied to drunks and unemployables. In the 1870's separate wings where added for African Americans, as it was segregated.

When construction was finished in 1880, the hospital was already holding 500 more patients than it was built to house. The conditions began to deteriorate quickly, not only to the building but also inside the building. The increase of patients was not accompanied with an increase in funding.

The staff was stretched thin. The constant need for nurses kept them from doing other but equally import tasks like cleaning. Grime built up on the once clear windows that let that healing sunlight in. Outbreaks of disease weren't uncommon.

Rooms built for one patient now housed five. People slept on floors and in hallways. In this type of environment, it only takes a few evil people to make everyone's life miserable. The asylum felt the need to segregate white and black patients but didn't feel that same need to keep child molesters away from children. A nurse also disappeared, she was found a few months later dead, at the bottom on as unused stairwell. Multiple other solved and unsolved murders happened here.

Several fires were started by patients. In one case, the nurse that stumbled on the fire did not want to pull the fire alarm and cause a panic, so she pulled the dinner bell. 390 patients calmly walked away from danger.

In 1935 a patient set fire to the north ward. That repair represents the only remodel that the asylum had. The fire destroyed the fourth floor. It cost $155.000 and was paid for by the Works Progress Administration. The hospital couldn't afford the repairs. A few years before in 1913, the hospital had been renamed the Weston State Hospital.

They used the same technics here as they did in St. Albans, with one terrifying addition. If you thought electric shock therapy was bad, wait till you meet its big brother, lobotomy. Enter Dr. Freeman.

Dr. Freeman was born in 1895. After graduating Yale, he got his medical degree in 1920 from the University of Pennsylvania. He traveled to Europe to study neurology. Upon his return he became the first neurologist in Washington DC.

It was during this time that Dr. Freeman first came in contact with mentally ill patients. He wanted to try and help them. He began experimenting with oxygen therapy and chemical treatments.

In 1935 he read about a technic being tested on animals. By removing small parts of a chimpanzee's frontal lobe, their poor behavior seemed corrected. That same year a doctor in Portugal began performing "Leucotomy" on patients.

The thought behind this was an excess of emotions caused mental illness. By removing part of the frontal lobe, the patients would stabilize the patient's personality.

Dr. Freeman modified the procedure and renamed it a lobotomy. He then performed the first lobotomy in America on a 63 year old woman who suffered from insomnia and depression. He drilled six holes in her head. After the surgery she was cured and lived another five years.

He performed more lobotomies and came up with a less invasive technic. Instead of drilling through skull, he would use electroshock to knock the patient out, then he would use the tools in the picture to the left. He would hammer an ice pick through their eye and severe their frontal lobe.

Instead of curing this often left patients in a child like state, or worse vegetative. Regardless of not curing the patients, lobotomies became common practice, solely because after a lobotomy, patients were much easier to handle.

Dr. Freeman toured the country showing doctors how to perform them. He personally performed 2,900 lobotomies, and 19 of those where on children under 18.

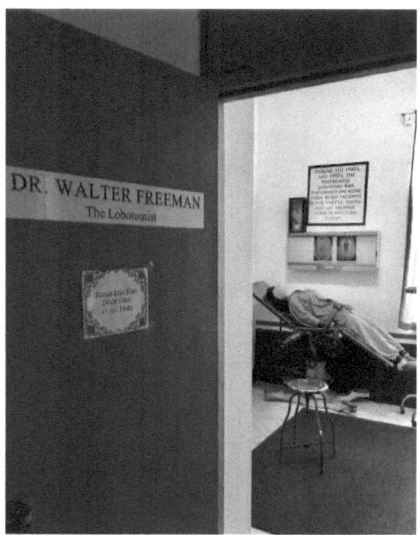

In the 40's and 50's 40,000 lobotomies where performed in the US. 490 of those patients died. He is responsible for a few of those deaths. He even killed a man during an exhibition on lobotomy with a large media presence attending.

When Dr. Freeman would arrive here, patients would hide, and he would roam the halls selecting people at random. In 1952 he claims to have performed 250 lobotomies in 12 days while touring West Virginia mental hospitals. He performed his last lobotomy in 1967, that patient died three days later.

The farm had been built to be able to feed more people than the asylum was built to hold, but only for 50 more. Built for 250 people it was now holding 1,500 people. The stocks were stretched thin, patients began to get malnourished.

The stress of starvation wasn't helping anyone's mental health. The nurses couldn't control the patients and pandemonium ensued.

In 1949 the Charleston Gazette went to investigate the asylum, currently at 1,800 patients. The story they published shocked the public and they began calling for it to be shut down.

The reporters had written about how they had seen unruly patients locked in cages or chained to walls to protect staff and other patients. They had witnessed the lack of building maintenance, like how the heat didn't work. Wallpaper was peeling off on its own when the patients weren't pulling it off.

The reporters saw people whose lives have been irreversibly damaged by lobotomies and other treatments they had received. they wandered the same halls that they had for decades. Those same patents were forced to sleep on the cold floors of the hallway because there was neither beds nor space to put the beds. Each bedroom had 5 or 6 patients sleeping in it, most on the floor.

The fourth floor of the north wing was reported to be luxurious though, after it's rebuild 14 years before. It was still overcrowded, like the rest of the hospital.

Although politicians made promises to shut it down occurred no action ever followed.

While lobotomies where being performed with reckless disregard in the 1950's, that decade also set another milestone for the asylum. Their population had peaked. 2,600 patients called it home. That's more than 10 times the original amount of people it was built to hold.

A change was coming to state institutions.

On Staten Island, New York City sat Willow Brook State School. It housed 5,000 children and adults with learning disabilities. In 1965 Senator Robert Kennedy toured it and called it overcrowded with people living in filth and dirt, their clothes in rags. The rooms as comfortable and cheery as the cages we keep animals in at the zoo. He plead for change

Donna Stone was an advocate for the treatment of the mentally ill and learning disabled. She posed as a social worker applying for a job and spent several days working in the back ward. The conditions were worse than she imagined, and she went to the press. Multiple stories where published about it.

A doctor at Willow Brook named Michael Wilkins had urged parents of children there to organize and protest to demand better conditions. The first reporter to publish a story about the school was Jane Kurtin. While covering the protest she met two social workers who worked there and let her in. She witnessed the horrible conditions firsthand. Dr. Wilkins was then fired.

Dr. Wilkins returned the favor by contacting Geraldo Rivera, a local investigative reporter who went there and Dr. Wilkins let him in the back door. He also went to another state school. The nightly news ran at 10 part series with his shocking footage. Words can't describe it, it's a little traumatic. It is a visual depiction of how many state hospitals were.

It received nation recognition and Geraldo won a Peabody award. Its called Willow Brook, our last great disgrace, it's on YouTube.

Using his footage as evidence parents of children in Willow Brook filled a $500 million class action lawsuit in federal court that same year. That case is called New York ARC vs Rockefeller. ARC stands for Association of Retarded Citizens.

In 1975 a judgment was signed by the courts that ordered the state of New York to improve the conditions in Willow Brook, specifically reduce the overpopulation and add programing as the children sat unattended and unstimulated all day.

28 states where sued over the treatment in state institutions. Those rulings began shaping federal law. Everything from patient being individually funded with Medicaid to a new emphasis on community housing over large institutions. What would qualify someone for commitment changed and began an emphasis on short term care. Special education programs also started in schools.

In 1980 congress passed the Civil Rights of Institutional Persons Act. It covered all facilities of state placement. From mental health facilities to public nursing homes, to jails and prisons. It did not grant any new rights but enforces the already provided rights granted by the constitution.

In 1982, 10 years after the original report, Geraldo Rivera had gotten a nice promotion and was a correspondent on 20/20, went back. He brought with him Bernard, a former patient who was misdiagnosed with a learning disorder when he really had cerebral palsy. He was in Willow Brook for 18 years. 10 years later he's on the consumer advisory board helping to monitor changes at the institution.

Bernard had his own set of keys, so there was no need to sneak in the back door, but to keep them honest Geraldo would show up a day early or a day late of his scheduled visit to catch them off guard.

He caught construction crews hurriedly repairing the building and pressure washing it. The other school he went to didn't do much better, he caught them bringing back patients they had hidden. Both the schools were much better than before though, Willow Brook then only had 1,300 patients, compared to 5,000 during the first series.

In 1985 the Charleston Gazette returned to the Weston State School after its court mandated inspectors called it "dirty and unkempt with patients left naked and confined to dirty wards. The population of the Asylum was aging with new patients being sent to other facilities.

In 1994 the patients were sent to a new facility and the governor planned on converting it to a prison. That plan didn't happen and neither did any of the future plans for the building.

Over 50,000 people are buried in the cemetery, so many that they had to expand the grounds making the total acreage 666 acres.

In 2007 the campus was auctioned and bought for 1.5 million by an asbestos removal contractor called Joe Jordan. In 2008 it opened for tours. It has returned to being the biggest employer in town, and has been featured on multiple ghost shows.

SWEET SPRINGS SANATORIUM

At the base of Pete's mountain is a spring. The water is naturally carbonated and is 75 degrees all year round. The water has so much calcium, magnesium, potassium and zinc that by modern standard it can be sold as a health drink.

To the left is part of the bath, the spring naturally fills it. It was built in 1830. Unfortunate part of the bath house was dismantled, and the bricks sold. There's also a monster snapping turtle that calls this pool home.

In 1774 James Moss found these springs. He was the first white man to see it. He claimed the land, later giving his claim to William Lewis. In 1774 Mr. Lewis moved here with his family.

By the 1790's Mr. Lewis had built a hotel out of stone and several log cabins. It totaled 72 rooms and guests flocked to drink the healing waters. To the left is the chimney of the original hotel, not much more remains of it

It saw many celebrity guests like George and Martha Washington. Constitution signers like Patrick Henry (give me liberty or give me death) and James Madison our 4th president also checked in here.

In 1805 James Lewis divided up his land between his sons. He gave 400 acres, that included sweet springs to his son john.

John Lewis had been a colonel in the Virginia Militia during the revolutionary war. After the war he became a doctor.

William wanted his son to build a town around the springs and like a good son, that's what he did.

The Grand hotel was built in 1839 by John Lewis. It is (currently) 110,000 square feet. Local legend says that it was designed by Thomas Jefferson, but new research says it was designed by Thomas Jefferson's co-worker William Phillips.

The front of the hotel is 250 feet wide. The dining room was 160 feet long. There were 36 bedrooms upstairs. The basement had a kitchen, a bar and two reception rooms. There were also rooms designed to lock slaves in so they couldn't run away.

The hotel's popularity boomed before the civil war. The whole resort could house over 800 people. The stream of celebrities continued. The rich and powerful came here to rub shoulders. Chief Justice John Marshal and: Senator, Representative, 7th Speaker of the house and 9th Secretary of State Henry Clay stayed here. In all, 6 US presidents would stay here.

I mentioned Dr Burke in Yellow Sulphur Springs. He's the doctor whose books began the healing Springs Resorts popularity. In his 1846 book named "Guidebook to Mineral Springs", he said "Patients could live to the fabled age of the crow, bathing in the Sweet Springs".

In 1852 John Lewis was in so much debt that the hotel was sold to Oliver Bernie. Mr. Bernie split the land between his brother Christopher and Senator Allen T. Caperton. They formed the Sweet Springs Company.

The resort closed during the Civil War. In 1864 the Union Army camped here. It reopened after the war but never to its previous glory. Celebrity guests were still making appearances, including Queen Victoria, General Beauregard and Robert E. Lee. Robert E. Lee was such a believer in the healing powers of the spring water that he sent his horse "Traveler" here for treatments.

The buildings in the pictures were also used to house guest. They were called the seven sisters. There aren't seven buildings left anymore but the one above has been renovated and is used as the office.

The end of the Civil War marked the boom of the railroad industry. Part of that boom consisted of hauling coal out of the West Virginia coal fields. Sweet Springs is in Monroe county, and there is no coal in Monroe. No railroads were ever laid to Monroe county. The more rail travel became common, the fewer guests where taking the long trip by road. The resort closed in 1928. Multiple attempts to reopen it failed. In the picture to the Left is the Caldwell house. It was a stagecoach stop for guests of Sweet Springs.

In 1941 Sweet Springs was owned by D.M. Tailer of Roanoke Virginia. He sold it to the state of West Virginia. They remodeled it and used it as a tuberculosis sanitarium. Two large wings in the back of the building where added.

In 1945 it became the "Andrew S. Rowan Home for the Elderly", Andrew Rowan was a war hero from Monroe county who had died a few years earlier in 1942. He had earned a Distinguished Service Cross in the Spanish American War. Odds are the first residents of the nursing home knew him.

The nursing home closed in 1993. Monroe county was given the land by the state. The county planned on turning the resort into a drug rehab. They borrowed 1.3 million dollars, but the rehab never occurred and the county defaulted on the loan.

The land, now only 23 acres passed through multiple hands, but the hotel remained unused. One of the owners had hired Raymond Herlong to renovate the hotel. Coincidentally, his great aunt was married to John Lewis, who had originally built the hotel in 1839.

In 1997 Ashby Berkley got Sweet Springs put on the Historic registry. Back in 1986 he had bought another healing springs resort. He restored it and ran it as an Inn until 2001. He then sold it to the state who turned it into a female prison. In 2015 he bought Sweet Springs with plans of restoring it.

GHOST TOWNS OF THURMOND AND GLEN JEAN

This isn't the story about two towns, but the men who owned the towns and really just hated each other. Captain William Dabney Thurmond owned the land on the north side of the New River, and Thomas G. McKell owned the land on the southside. Both towns are in the New River Gorge in Fayette county West Virginia.

Captain Thurmond was born in 1820 in Amherst county Virginia and moved to Fayette county with his father's family in 1845. During the Civil war he was a captain in a Militia called Thurmond's Rangers. He fought for the south and participated in local guerilla warfare. He wasn't the namesake of Thurmond's Rangers; his brother Phillip Thurmond was. Phillip was killed in 1874 in Putnam county West Virginia.

In 1873 the Chesapeake and Ohio (C and O) railroad commissioned Thurmond to do some surveying work and paid him 73 acres of land instead of cash. As the railroad was built a stop was put on his land and a small community grew. He operated a ferry across the river, to the land owned by Thomas McKell.

Thomas McKell owned a large swath of coal and timer rich land but with no connection to the railroad, it was nearly worthless. The railroad was the only way in and out of the New River Gorge. The rails where only on the north side of the river, he was on the south side. In 1870 he founded a town on his side of the River. He named it Glen Jean in honor of his wife Jean.

In 1889 Mr. McKell negotiated with the C and O railroad and a bridge was built across the river. It crossed from Thurmond to Glen Jean. This bridge unlocked the untouched coal and timber resources on the south side of the river. In 1893 Mr. McKell started the McKell Coal and Coke company. He paid his workers in company script.

Every train coming from the south side of the river passed through Thurmond and Glen Jean and the boom was on. Thurmond opened a general store and built 30 houses to rent. In 1891 he built the Hotel Thurmond. In 1898 it burned down and was rebuilt of brick, reopening in 1901. That same year Mr. McKell opened his hotel in Glen Jean, it was called the Glen Dunn, was 4 stories tall and had 100 rooms.

Thurmond was a bible thumping Baptist who banned gambling and alcohol in his town. He could look across the river and see the nonstop part and the Glen Dunn hotel. In 1903 both Thurmond and McKell incorporated their towns. They were both scared the other would try and incorporate the other's town as part of theirs. Mr. McKell died the next year in 1904.

Thurmond also operated The Thurmond Coal company. His town also held two other mining companies' offices. They also had 3 general stores, a post office, a western union office, a jewelry store and 2 banks. In 1910 Thurmond was the number one stop for the C and O railroad with 75,000 passengers that year. Thurmond also died that year.

In 1914 prohibition put the brakes on the good time at the Glean Dunn hotel. Then in 1915 a flood wiped out the bridge connecting the 2 town. Thurmond was inaccessible by road and Glean Jean was inaccessible by rail. The bridge was reopened in 2 years later in 1917.

In 1922 a large fire burned down most of the town of Glen Jean and in 1930 the Glen Dunn hotel burned down. Thurmond also suffered a fire in the 1930's. The economy began to turn bad and two banks, a hotel and a phone company office closed. In 1956 the trains stopped using the New River Gorge line.

Buildings continued to be abandoned as the population declined. In 1995 the post office closed. That's when the park service stepped in. They renovated the train depot and turned it into a visitor's center, to the left.

In 2010 Thurmond had 7 residents. In 2016 it had 5. Now the post office is closed but since the park service is there, it's not a real ghost town... but getting closer.

THE LEGEND OF JOHN HENRY

The legend of John henry is American folklore which unlike Pecos Bill and Paul Bunyan has its roots firmly planted in the truth. Most of what we know about John Henry comes from research done by Guy B. Johnson. He was born in 1901 in Texas. From 1927 to 1969 he was a professor at the University of North Carolina. As a black man he was interested in his history, and he came to Monroe county West Virginia to see the tunnel where John Henry raced the steam driven machine and interviewed witnesses who had watched. Although there are multiple theories on John Henry, his is mostly likely the most accurate.

John Henry was born in 1840's as a slave and was freed after the civil war. He relocated to Virginia to find work in the reconstruction effort. In Virginia he was arrested for burglary and sentence to the state penitentiary. It was a large white building that rose above the city skyline.

The warden of the penitentiary was a Quaker from Pennsylvania. He had been appointed to his position as part of the reconstruction effort and he was shocked by the horrible conditions there. His reaction to the conditions was to save the inmates from having to live in the penitentiary by leasing them as labor to private contractors. He later became as opponent of inmate labor.

John Henry was leased to the Chesapeake and Ohio Railroad (C and O). He was a giant of a man, standing over 6 foot and weighing in at over 200 pounds. His strength was legendary. The workers would often sing to help keep cadence as they swung their hammers. They would often make up their own songs about each other and these songs began the legend of John Henry. The songs spoke of his superhuman strength like how he could swing a 20-pound hammer in each hand. Other songs described his softer side, like being kindhearted and having good morals.

By the time the railroad reached the Great Bend mountain, John Henry was the leader of his work crew. Leveling grade and laying track turned into driving holes into the rock, which would then be stuffed full of dynamite, and the rocks blown up and hauled away. The Great Bend tunnel is 6,450 feet long and was completed in 1872.

The famous story about John Henry happened here in 1870. The C and O railroad had used a steam drill at the nearby Lewis Tunnel. John Henry was impressed when he saw the machine and challenged it to a race. When the dust cleared after the hour long contest, the drill had only gone 9 feet while John Henry had gone 14 feet. It was reported that the steam drill had hit a seam of harder rock which had cost it time.

In 1929 Guy B. Johnson interviewed witnesses to the race. Most of the men agreed that John Henry didn't die after the race, but later in a rock side or of disease. The last time that John Henry was noted in documents from the Virginia State Penitentiary was in 1873. This was before his sentence discharge date and there is no record of a pardon.

He might have passed on, but legends don't die. As time passed the men of his work crew moved on to different crews and different locations, but they never stopped singing. Westward expansion was in full effect and 1,000's of miles of track needed to be laid, and they always needed a man who could swing a hammer. Soon John Henry was the hero of the track layers. They loved to sing about him and now people who had never met him were making up songs about him. These songs began to blur the lines between fact and fantasy.

The early 1900's began the Jazz age. Multiple jazz songs where written about him. Some of those songs were recorded onto records. Records weren't new technology, but they had become much accessible to the public by then.

One of those songs about John Henry ends with; They took him to the white house and buried him in the sand, every train that goes by says there lays a steel driving man. John Henry was pretty cool, but he wasn't bury him in the front yard of the president's house cool. Who is, right? Plus, the soils not sandy and there aren't any train lines close to it. It was assumed there was a few creative liberties taken with the song.

Many years later the Virginia State Penitentiary was taken out of use and torn down. It was sitting on valuable land in Richmond and the city was eager to develop it. The large white building surrounded by an imposing wall had been part of the city's skyline for over 100 years. As the land was excavated, multiple mass graves were dug up out of the sandy soil. Richmond has sandy soil and a railroad nearby as the song said. It is completely possible that John Henry was one of the men in those graves.

THE CARROLL COUNTY COURTHOUSE MASSACRE

This is Sidna Allen's house. He built his dream home in 1911 but never got to live in it. Located in Carroll county, Virginia, at the foothills of the Blue Ridge mountains. During a time that every farm had a still, and family ties ran stronger than the law, trouble brewed.

It all started the year before during a corn shucking. When the crops came in it was the tradition for the families to help each other out and have parties where they pulled the husks off the corn. If you peeled an ear of corn and it was red, you got to get a kiss from the girl of your choice. And so, it happened, with the moonshine flowing, an Allen boy got a kiss from a girl another boy was courting, and he didn't take kindly to it. They took it behind the barn and two of the Allen boys got the best of the other boy. He swore a warrant out on them, so they ran off to the next county, which happened to be in North Carolina.

They lay low working in a quarry near Mount Airy. Due to mounting political pressure, the Surry county Sheriff picked up the boys and brought them back to Virginia, with a Carroll county Sheriff deputy meeting him at the state line. That deputy wasn't to gentle with the boys, some say dragging them behind the horse.

Sidna's brother Floyd saw this. Floyd was a landowner and as most respectable men were, he had been deputized (so the sheriff could round up a posse). He offered to take the boys to jail himself but was refused. Maybe the deputy felt insulted by this offer, or maybe he thought one of the Allen's couldn't be trusted to take another Allen to jail. He might have been right because Floyd's reaction to this was to pistol whip the deputy with his own gun and release the boys on the condition they turned themselves into the Sheriff.

As no good deed goes unpunished, Floyd Allen was charged with assaulting the deputy in his line of duty. Floyd was furious, and swore he wouldn't serve a day in jail, moreover, he would kill anyone involved in the proceedings. He was only protecting two young boys being abused. The county was in an uproar. Two Allens even became deputies to intimidate witnesses.

The day of the trial was tense. Floyd was a man of his word, so the judge and commonwealth attorney came to court armed. The Sheriff was there with some deputies too. Floyd also had a gun, so did his brother Sidna and a whole lot of other Allens behind him. Guilty, but only a year in prison.

Moments later the room was filled with smoke and shot. Frank made his escape with his clan and ran out into the street. More sheriff deputies and private citizens were waiting for him. A second shoot out raged. Floyd was hit and taken to a local hotel, but not Sidna. He and those who could, scattered up into the hills to hide.

5 people were killed and 7 injured in the shootout, including the judge, the sheriff, the prosecutor, multiple deputies, witnesses and jurors. Virginia law says that if a sheriff dies, the deputies lose power until a new sheriff can be sworn in, so the national guard was called in to restore order.

In the picture to the right, a bullet hole from the shootout in the center of the second step.

Within a year, all the participants of the shoot out where caught by the long arm of the law. Floyd and his son where both sent to the chair. Sidna and his son made it all the way out to Iowa, but the Baldwin-Felts detectives still found them. Sidna was given 35 years but was pardoned by the governor. He lost his house and land as part of his sentence. Because of the notoriety of his case, he was able to make a living working in a side show. People paying a dime to see a survivor of the Carroll county massacre.

In the picture to the left, the third step has a bullet hole from the shootout.

This story was nationwide headline news...until the titanic sank.

The Sidna Allen house fell into disrepair but is how being restored by The Friends of J. Sidna Allen House.

The picture to the right is the view as they ran out of the courthouse. Imagine the street lined with sheriff's deputies and the air full of bullets and smoke.

THE ROANOKE ALMS HOUSE

In the days before social welfare, if you couldn't provide for yourself you could be civilly committed to a poor house. Its residents where called inmates. Its true purpose ranged from an orphanage, to an old folks' home, to housing for mothers and children with nowhere to go. Before JFK made food stamps in 1960, these were the governments only programs to help poverty. This is the Roanoke poorhouse.

The residents didn't like the name poor house and called it the Alms house. Alms or Alms giving means to giving to others as an act of virtue or charity. The word is incredibly old and dates to the ancient Greeks, then later into old English.

The original Alms house was built in 1884 on the northwest side of town. In 1888 the property values increased, and it was sold for $13,000. The city purchased Jacob Persinger's 200-acre farm for $16,000 on the south side of town.

John Long is the director of the Salem museum, Salem is a Roanoke suburb. He has done extensive research on the alms house. He has never found a firsthand account of the original alms house, but he told the Roanoke Times "The conditions there would have been deplorable. It was a safety net for those with nowhere else to go. For the homeless or someone who couldn't take care of themselves or the sick, this was the best and only care you could get".

The Original Alms house built on Persinger's farm opened in 1890. It was on the east side of the road, then it was called Poor House Road, now it's called Colonial Ave. On the west side of the road was a hospital for people with smallpox. The residents worked the 200-acre farm and produced their own food. There was also a diary on the farm, and they sold milk to the Clover Creamery in Roanoke.

Between 1918 and 1921 there was an influenza epidemic. 76 of the 118 residents died. In the 1920's a local woman's group toured the alms house and where shocked by what they saw. Their account described it as a disease-ridden house of horrors and made it sound like something out of a Charles Dickens novel. Historic accounts make it sound like the best thing that ever happened to the Roanoke alms house is when it burnt down in 1925. No one was hurt.

That same year it was rebuilt with bricks and still stands. It is the only building left standing of the entire complex. In the 1930's Biddle and Annie Doss became the caretakers. With their arrival began the better treatment of the residents. They lived in a small white cottage on the property with their two sons, Clovis and James.

It functioned as the alms house until 1957. From 1890 to 1957, 2400 people lived here and half of them died here. The last person to die here was a 2-day old girl. Nothing is known about her except here last name was Williams and she was buried in grave 545. In 1959 it was leased to the Jerome Natt School for retarded children (their words not mine). By 1959 the city was trying to sell the land.

The Roanoke technical institute operated on the eastside of the road, it was a branch of Virginia Tech. On the west side of the road was the University of Virginia. In 1966 they merged to form the Virginia Western Community College. During this transition they acquired the Alms house property. The cemetery was moved to Coyer Springs in the nearby town of Fincastle.

The building is now called The Thomas Center for Advanced studies. The building isn't on the historic registry but when the schools merged, they renovated and kept it. Its presence is now a memorial. A hidden memorial with no signs or plaques, but still a memorial.

Psst, wanna see a real ghost town?

REAL GHOST TOWN OF LIGNITE

This is the main street in downtown Lignite. This is Botetourt county Virginia, in the Jefferson National Forest. Thurmond is in a national park; the park service maintains it. No one maintains Lignite. Lignite had a post office and a zip code, it now has neither of those. Currently the population is zero.

Lignite was founded in the late 1800's by the Allegheny Ore and Iron company, the town of was named after the type of coal they mined. Lignite is a low quality coal and is called brown coal.

In the 1920's a better vein of coal was found in Coachville, PA. The company disassembled many of the buildings including a church, theater, library, school, a company store and the post office. They reassembled them in Coachville. In Pennsylvania they operated under the name Lukens Steel company.

Some houses where left and people took them over. The town became populated again by people living in abandoned homes. In 1950 the land became part of the Jefferson national forest. The park service came in and forced them out. Since then the woods have reclaimed.

KIDNAPPED BY THE CIRCUS

During my research I read an article were a niece of the Muse Brothers was very insistent that the brothers be properly respected and call mister, so I will do just that. Mr. Wille was born in 1892 and his brother Mr. George was born in 1893. The brothers were black Albinos. The odds of a child being born albino is 1 in 10,000, having two children born albino is very rare. The brothers were born to a family of poor sharecroppers in Franklin county Virginia.

In 1899, they were working in their family's tobacco fields when a talent scout/bounty hunter kidnapped them. His name was James "Candy" Shelton. He told them that their mother (Harriet) was dead and sold them to a circus side show.

To accentuate their appearance the brother grew their blond hair into long dreadlocks. First, they were called "The White Ecuadorian Cannibals, then "The Sheep Headed Men", and later "The Ambassadors from Mars" who had crashed their spaceship into the Mojave Desert.

They were also musicians and entertained by playing the mandolin. During this time, they worked for the Al G. Barnes Circus. The brothers were sold between circus's, they were never paid a salary but were always given room and board and cared for by the circus. By the 1920's they were touring with the Ringling Brother and Barnum and Baily Circus.

In October 1927 the brother's mom had a dream telling her to go to the circus in Roanoke. She went and sitting in the front row she saw her boys for the first time in 28 years. Just as she saw them, they saw her, and tried to leave with her. The circus wasn't having that, and the police were called. The circus's lawyers argued that the brothers had to stay with the circus.

The Roanoke Commonwealth Attorney was also a founding member of the Roanoke chapter of the KKK and Mrs. Harriet was an illiterate maid, but that didn't stop her and in true American fashion she found a lawyer and sued the circus three days later. Since the brothers had never been handed a paycheck, they sued for $100,000 in back pay. They got a much smaller amount, but did get a much better contract, including monthly pay with some of that pay sent to their parents. Their brother, Mr. Tom was also hired by the circus. Another change to the contract lets the brothers sell merchandise and keep the profits. From that time on Mrs. Harriet kept a lawyer and bail bondsman on retainer to guaranty her boy's safety and well being.

The next year they returned to show business, working for the Dreamland circus and side show. Their first season back they were playing in Madison Square Garden, drawing 10,000 people per performance. During the 1930's they tour Europe, even performing for the queen of England. In 1937 they returned to America and began touring with the "Ringling Brothers and Barnum and Baily Circus". The brothers saved up money and bought their dear mother a house in Roanoke.

In 1961 they retired, ending their career with the Clyde Beatty Circus. They returned home to Virginia and lived together in the house they had bought their mother. 10 years later in 1971 Mr. George died. His brother, Mr. WIllie lived until the ripe age of 108. He died on Good Friday 2001. They are buried at Williams Memorial Cemetery in Roanoke.

THE FRANKLIN COUNTY MOONSHINE CONSPIRACY

Before prohibition, alcohol taxes made up 30-40% of Government revenue. Prohibition was the 18th amendment of the constitution and banned the sale of alcohol from 1919 to 1933. Prohibition didn't stop the production of liquor, it just changed who the taxes were paid to.

Franklin County Virginia was called the wettest county in the world. Its most northern town is Boones Mill. During prohibition it was where rum runners consolidate their loads for distribution to distant markets, earning it the nickname The Moonshine Capital of the World.

Deputy Prohibition Commissioner N. C. Alexander said of Franklin county "Of the 30,000 residents of Franklin county, 29,999 of them are mixed up in the illegal whisky business." From 1930 to 1935 Franklin county used 34 million pounds of sugar, which pound for pound was more than New York City used during that same time span. They also went through 13 million pounds of corn meal, 1 million pounds of malt, 30,300 pounds of hops and 35 million pounds of yeast. Franklin county produced 500 to 1,000 gallons of white lightning daily. The taxes not paid on Franklin county moonshine would have been $5.5 million, $95.6 million today.

Making alcohol is an old tradition, brought by the Scots and Irish. They were the first European settlers to come to Franklin county. Every farm had a still, not just for consumption but for sanitation and medical treatments. Farmers also found shipping a bushel of corn to market costs much less when that corn had been converted to alcohol.

Coming out of the Great Depression, Prohibition offered the residents of Franklin county a chance to make easy money, fast. Soon more than just moonshiners were profiting, with local officials demanding protection money.

The shiners were charged $25 or $30 a month. Not only would that buy the Sherriff looking the other way but when the feds would come knocking, he would lead them off course and have them chasing their tails. This was called the Granny Fee system.

Sheriff J. P. Hodges is credited with starting the Granny Fees system. When he died in office, his son Wilson Hodges took over as Sheriff. During the next election for Sheriff, Cornelius Jamison's supporters would leave cards on liquor stills destroyed by the law. The card would say "This still destroyed by Wilson Hodges, Vote Jamison. Cornelius Jamison was elected sheriff in 1932. He remained the sheriff until he was indicted in 1935.

Unique times produce unique characters. There was Mrs. Willie Carter, the queen of Roanoke bootleggers. She claimed to have moved 220,000 gallons of hooch between 1926 and 1931. There were also the Bondurant brothers, who owned a local filling station. They weren't known for their mass alcohol production as much as their reputation for being invincible. The movie "Lawless" was based on them and was based on The Great Franklin County Moonshine Conspiracy written by Jack Bondurant's grandson, Matt Bondurant.

Unlike in the movie the Bondurant brothers did pay protection money. Federal Agent Rake from the movie was also a real person. Sent to Franklin County to enforce prohibition he was soon profiting from it. He was a bit of a dandy and despised the country folk of Franklin county, which made enforcing the Granny fee system easier for him. The only thing true about the final scene is that there was a shoot out on a bridge and that Rakes shot two of the brothers. The how and why of the movie are Hollywood magic.

A total of 34 Franklin county residents were federally indicted for the bribery scheme. Including 19 moonshiners, one corporation, and 9 government officials. The government officials included the commonwealth attorney, his name was Charles Carter Lee and he was a great nephew to Robert E. Lee. There were also 4 sheriff's deputies, a former member of the General Assembly and a federal prohibition officer (Rakes) indicted. There were also 55 unindicted co-conspirators (Bondurants).

7 pled guilty, including Wilson Hodges. 7 more pleaded no contest. The remaining 20 went to trial. The trial started in April 1935 and lasted 10 weeks with 176 witnesses testifying. The trial was in the federal court house in Roanoke and was the second longest trial in Virginia history.

One day before he was set to testify, a Franklin County Sheriff's deputy who had been the treasurer of the Granny Fee system was shot to death. Deputy Richards was on a prisoner transport. The man in the backseat had minutes before been arrested for petty theft from his boss. On Callaway Road two cars came speeding up behind him. As they passed him, one car opened fire with a 12-gauge shotgun, the other car was firing 45's at him. The cars turned around and headed back to the police car. Deputy Richards exited the vehicle and returned fire but was out gunned. The prisoner also exited the vehicle and fled into the woods. When the bodies were found, combined they had over 100 gunshot wounds. Another witness died of pneumonia before he could testify.

The jury was only out for 3 days. All were convicted except for 2 deputies and the Commonwealth Attorney, Lee. The sentences were light. 2 years in jail was the longest sentence given, with most of the defendants receiving probation. But things aren't ever that simple. Soon after the trial, word got out that a juror wouldn't convict anyone unless Commonwealth Attorney Lee was acquitted. In 1946 a new round of indictments came out. 24 people were indicted with jury tampering. 22 of them were convicted.

In 1937 Paul and Hubbard Duling of Nicholas county West Virginia where convicted of the murder of Deputy Richards and another murder in neighboring Roanoke county. The Roanoke county murder was very similar to the Franklin county slaying. The Duling brothers killed Roanoke Deputy Clarence Simons because they blamed him for the death of their brother while he was in his custody. When the brothers were first arrested in West Virginia, they were held in the jail in Beckley. The state of Virginia had to speedily extradite the brother because of rumors that a mob of their family members were preparing to break them out of jail. It took three trials but the brothers where handed 99 years in the Virginia State Penitentiary.

The transcripts from the first trial disappeared. A lawyer named T. Greer from Rocky Mount (the county seat of Franklin county) has been looking for them. He has written the families of the lawyers involved in the conspiracy trial looking for unknown copies. The last known location of the records was when they were sent to the federal courthouse in Harrisonburg Virginia in 1945. The records from the 1946 jury tampering trial have also disappeared.

MAGGODEE CREEK BRIDGE MASSACRE, FRANKLIN COUNTY, VIRGINIA

On 12/19/1930 Jack and Forest Bondurant were both driving vehicles filled with homemade liquor. They were stopped by Sheriff Deputy Absire and Federal prohibition officer Rakes at the bridge. They demanded that the Bondurants turn over a carload of liquor.

Forest reminded the deputies that he had already paid his monthly bribe, but they were having none of it. To prevent the deputies from taking his car, Jack (the youngest of the brothers) threw his Ford's keys into the creek. Deputy Rakes responded by shooting Jack in the stomach. When Forest ran to his brother's aid, Deputy Rakes fired on him too, and hit him in the arm.

The oldest brother Howard arrived on the scene Deputy Rakes fires on him too, but Deputy Absire knocked the gun, making him miss. Howard took Jack to the hospital in Rocky Mount, Deputy Absire did the same with Forest. That left Deputy Rakes alone with two carloads of shine. He impounded the cars and when they arrived in Rocky Mount 30 gallons of hooch was discovered. The brothers said they left home with 120 gallons.

Years later, when Matt Bondurant found the newspaper account of these advents, he asked his grandfather, Jack if it was true. Jack Bondurant didn't speak a word, he only pulled up his shirt, showing the scars he got that day.

Thanks to all who preserve history

Refrences

yellowsulfursprings.com

spec.lib.vt.edu

loc.gov

Virginia.org

Virginia.gov

Coalcampusa.com

Archive.org

Realmccoycabins.com

Csa-railroads.com

Civilwar.vt.edu

Newspaper.com

Peidmontparanormalsociety.org

Mayoclinic.org

Abandonedspaces.com

Asyllumproject.org

Appomattoxcountyva.gov

Pocahontasva.org

Factfinder.census.gov

Coalcampusa.com

Bdtonline.com

Bramwellwv.com

Bestplaces.net

Forgottenlegacywwi.org

Opacity.us

Medicalbag.com

Legendsofamerica.com

Willow Brook

Willow Brook 2

Roanoke Times

Allthatsinteresting.com

Fincastleherald.com

True Vine by Beth Macy

The Wettest County in the World by Matt Bonurant.